SUPERNATURAL PROVISION

LIVING IN THE REALM OF GOD'S SUPERABUNDANCE

GLORIA COPELAND & PASTOR GEORGE PEARSONS

© 2014 Eagle Mountain International Church Inc. aka Kenneth Copeland Ministries. All rights reserved. No part of this book may be reproduced or transmitted in any form or by any means, electronic or mechanical, including photocopying, recording, or by any information storage and retrieval system, without the written permission of the publisher.

For more information about Kenneth Copeland Ministries, visit kcm.org or call 1-800-600-7395 (U.S. only) or +1-817-852-6000.

ISBN 978-1-60463-269-9
30-0834

Unless otherwise noted, all scripture is from the *King James Version* of the Bible.

Scripture quotations marked AMP are from *The Amplified Bible, Old Testament* © 1965, 1987 by the Zondervan Corporation. *The Amplified New Testament* © 1958, 1987 by The Lockman Foundation. Used by permission.

Scripture quotations marked NIV are from *The Holy Bible, New International Version* © 1973, 1978, 1984, 2011 by Biblica Inc. Used by permission. All rights reserved worldwide.

Scripture quotations marked MSG are from *The Message* © 1993, 1994, 1995, 1996, 2000, 2001, 2002. Used by permission of NavPress Publishing Group.

Scripture quotations marked NLT and NLT-96 are from the *Holy Bible, New Living Translation* © 1996, 2004 by Tyndale Charitable Trust. Used by permission of Tyndale House Publishers.

Scripture quotations marked NKJV are from the *New King James Version* © 1982 by Thomas Nelson Inc.

Scripture quotations marked CEV are from the *Contemporary English Version* © 1991, 1992, 1995 by American Bible Society. Used by permission.

Day 1
Quote from Bill Winston, *The Supernatural Church*, © 2014 Bill Winston Ministries.

"21 Ways God Supplies" from George Pearsons, *50 Days of Prosperity Vol. 1* (Fort Worth, Kenneth Copeland Publications), Day #30.

Day 2
Excerpt from "The Word Is Our Supply" prophecy taken from the "Now, What About 2011?" prophecy, delivered by Kenneth Copeland on November 11, 2010, at the 2010 Washington, D.C. Victory Campaign, Woodbridge, Va.

"God's Great Storehouse" prophecy taken from the "What About 2012" prophecy, © 2011 Kenneth Copeland. All rights reserved.

Days 4-5
Quotations from *John Gill's Expositions of the Bible*, a work originally published in two parts: *An Exposition of the New Testament* (1746-8), and *An Exposition of the Old Testament* (1748-63), pages 745 and 754, public domain.

Day 6
Word from the Lord delivered by Kenneth Copeland on November 19, 2005, *50 Days of Prosperity Vol. 1* by George Pearsons (Fort Worth, Kenneth Copeland Publications), Day #7.

Day 7
Excerpts from "Supernatural Wealth Transfer" brochure by Bill Winston, © 2012 Bill Winston Ministries.

Day 8
"And I Will Bless You Beyond Your Means" prophecy delivered by Kenneth Copeland on July 9, 2007, at the 2007 West Coast Believers' Convention, Anaheim, Calif.

Day 9
Quotes from Gloria Copeland, *God's Will Is Prosperity* (Fort Worth, Kenneth Copeland Publications, 1978), chapter 3, "Divine Prosperity."

Quotes from Kenneth Copeland, Kenneth and Gloria Copeland, *From Faith to Faith—A Daily Guide to Victory* (Fort Worth: Kenneth Copeland Publications, 1992), November 13 devotion.

"The Secret to Supernatural Living" article by Kenneth Copeland, published in the April 2013 edition of the *Believer's Voice of Victory* magazine, © 2013 Eagle Mountain International Church Inc. aka Kenneth Copeland Ministries.

LIVING IN THE REALM OF GOD'S SUPERABUNDANCE

GLORIA COPELAND & PASTOR GEORGE PEARSONS

TABLE OF CONTENTS

DAY #1
    Faith for Supernatural Provision 5
    21 Ways God Supplies 9

DAY #2
    Our Supernatural Provider 11
    God's Great Storehouse 13

DAY #3
    The Circle of Supernatural Provision 15

DAY #4
    Supernatural Provision in the Old Testament—Part 1 19

DAY #5
    Supernatural Provision in the Old Testament—Part 2 23

DAY #6
    Supernatural Provision in the New Testament 27

DAY #7
    Supernatural Wealth Transfer 31

DAY #8
    Supernatural Debt Cancellation 35

DAY #9
    Receiving Your Supernatural House 39

DAY #10
    Agents of Supernatural Provision 43

SUPERNATURAL PROVISION CONFESSION 45

THE SECRET TO SUPERNATURAL LIVING 47

LIVING IN THE REALM OF GOD'S SUPERABUNDANCE

GLORIA COPELAND & PASTOR GEORGE PEARSONS

Faith for Supernatural Provision

DAY #1

A. **James 1:17—Faith for Supernatural Provision**

1. "Rejoice and renew your faith in the supernatural. For it is time for the words and the faith and the preaching that has gone on before us to come to pass and come to full maturity. We will stand up and say, 'Surely the Glory has come down.'"
   —Word from the Lord through Kenneth Copeland, Dec. 24, 2005

2. "Super-natural"
   a. *Super*—above, over, beyond, higher, surpassing; outside the natural realm.

   b. *Natural*—lower, below, limited to the earthly realm; conforming to the ordinary course of nature; something deduced by human reason alone rather than by divine revelation.

   c. *Supernatural*—something that takes place outside the natural world; above, over, higher and beyond the ordinary course of nature.

3. *Supernatural Provision*—an unlimited, overwhelming supply that comes from above.
   a. James 1:17 (AMP): "Every good gift and every perfect (free, large, full) gift is from above; it comes down from the Father of all [that gives] light."

   b. MSG: "Every desirable and beneficial gift comes out of heaven."

4. It comes when the situation, paycheck, economy, job market and others are saying, "There is no way to meet this need. It is humanly impossible."
   a. "There's no end to it, and no rationing of it." —Gloria Copeland

5. God has unusual ways and unlimited avenues of provision that supersede all natural limitations.

6. Faith gives access to the supernatural.

7. "If you put things off in time and are looking through the natural progression of time, you can't operate in the supernatural. The supernatural only operates by faith and faith is a higher law than time." —Bill Winston, *The Supernatural Church*

B. Ephesians 3:20-21—Living in the Realm of Superabundance

1. AMP: "Now to Him Who, by (in consequence of) the [action of His] power that is at work within us, is able to [carry out His purpose and] do superabundantly, far over and above all that we [dare] ask or think [infinitely beyond our highest prayers, desires, thoughts, hopes, or dreams]—To Him be glory in the church and in Christ Jesus throughout all generations forever and ever. Amen (so be it)."
    a. "Faith will bring your dreams to pass." —Gloria Copeland

2. AMP/GK/NIV: "God is able to do superabundantly, immeasurably more, quite beyond what is normal or regular, without limit and then some on top of that, exceeding abundantly above and infinitely beyond."

3. We are not limited to or affected by the natural realm.

4. Supernatural provision will un-fix a fixed income.

5. The Lord will supernaturally provide in ways we have never considered.
    a. See "21 Ways God Provides, 191 Scriptures," page 9.

C. Philippians 4:19—Where Does Supernatural Provision Come From?

1. But my God shall supply all your need according to His riches in glory by Christ Jesus.

2. The Glory of God is the presence of God, heavy with everything good.

3. AMP/GK: "My God will liberally supply, fill to the full, cram, furnish, satisfy, finish and complete all of your needs, employment, requirements, lack and business according to His riches, His wealth, His money and His possessions in Glory by Christ Jesus."

4. Supernatural provision supersedes the impossible.

5. "The supernatural takes us past the impossible, through the unbelievable, into the ridiculous. As God is bringing you into this supernatural, He's bringing you into a place where the supernatural is no longer an option, but it is going to be a requirement. For you to get what God has for you, it requires the supernatural." —Bill Winston, *The Supernatural Church*
    a. We access supernatural provision by faith.
    b. We can't operate in the supernatural if we put things off in time by looking through the veil of time and the natural progression of time.
    c. The supernatural only operates by faith—and faith is a higher law than time.
    d. Faith has only one time zone—*now!*

6. "We have already entered the supernatural environment that God has been looking for all these years." —Kenneth Copeland, July 1, 2014

7. "There are things available to you right now in the realm of the spirit,' saith The LORD, 'that are far beyond your ability to reason it out. So lay aside the reason. Raise up your faith; exercise your faith and gratitude toward Me and I'll show you things that will take your mind a while to grasp.'" —Word from the Lord through Kenneth Copeland, June 30, 2014

NOTES

NOTES

21 Ways God Supplies

191 Scriptures

1. Tithing
- Malachi 3:10
- Leviticus 27:30
- Deuteronomy 26:1-2
- Hebrews 7:8
- Genesis 14:19-20

2. Sowing and Reaping
- Twice-sown seed—John 6:11
- Sowing in famine—Genesis 26:1, 12-14
- Those who scatter—Proverbs 11:24-28
- Law of seedtime and harvest—Genesis 8:22; Mark 4:26-32
- Supernatural increase—Psalm 115:12-14
- Deuteronomy 16:15
- 1 Corinthians 3:6
- Psalm 62:10

3. The Law of Multiplication
- Multiplication—Genesis 9:7, 16:10, 17:16; 2 Corinthians 9:10
- Hundredfold return—Mark 4:20, 10:28-30; 2 Samuel 24:3
- One thousand times more—Deuteronomy 1:11; Isaiah 60:22
- Made thee a million—Ezekiel 16:7 (Heb. trans.)
- The double—Isaiah 61:7; Exodus 22:7; Job 42:10

4. Giving to the Poor
- Proverbs 19:17
- Proverbs 28:27
- Psalm 41:1
- Matthew 19:21
- James 2:15-16
- Daniel 4:27
- The poor giving to you—1 Kings 17:9

5. The Ministry
- Giving to the house of the Lord—Haggai 1:7-10; 1 Chronicles 29:17, 25, 28
- Listen to the prophet—2 Chronicles 20:20
- Partnership with ministries—1 Samuel 30:24-25; 2 Kings 4:8-10
- Listen to your pastor—Psalm 23:1; Jeremiah 3:15, 23:3-4
- Increased anointing in hands of ministry—John 6:11-13
- Apostle John's greatest desire—3 John 2
- Prophet's reward—Matthew 10:41
- Righteous man's reward—Matthew 10:41

6. Memorial Giving
- Mark 12:41-44
- Acts 10:4
- Matthew 26:13

7. Our Relationship With God
- Honoring and loving God—Proverbs 3:9-10, 8:17-21
- God's pleasure in us—Psalm 35:27; Luke 12:32
- By seeking Him first—Matthew 6:33-34; Job 22:21
- Being taught by God—Isaiah 48:17

8. Provision Direct From the Throne
- Seed for the sower—2 Corinthians 9:10
- The hand of God—1 Chronicles 29:14-16; Numbers 11:23
- God's own ability for us—Ephesians 3:20; 2 Corinthians 9:8
- Come to the throne—Hebrews 4:16
- Daily provision—Psalm 68:19; Exodus 16:4
- His riches in glory—Philippians 4:19; Ephesians 3:16
- Your heavenly account—Philippians 4:17-20; Matthew 6:19-21
- Wisdom—Proverbs 3:13-15, 4:5-9, 24:3-4

9. By Creation, Re-Creation and Restoration
- Creating something from faith—Genesis 1:1; Hebrews 11:1-3; Romans 4:17
- Creating something from very little—John 6:11; 1 Kings 17:13-14; 2 Kings 4:7; Luke 5:5-7
- Re-creation of a substance—John 2:7-10; Luke 3:8
- Supernatural restoration—Joel 2:25; Exodus 22:7; Proverbs 6:31

10. Miraculous Provision
- Debt Cancellation—Deuteronomy 15:1-2; Philemon 18-19; 1 Samuel 17:25, 22:2; 2 Kings 4:7, 6:5-6; Matthew 18:27, 6:12; Leviticus 25:10; Nehemiah 5:3-4, 11-12
- Reaping where you haven't sown—Leviticus 25:11; John 4:38

- Receiving what you didn't ask for—
  1 Kings 3:13
- Without money—Isaiah 55:1

11. Earth's Resources
- Psalm 24:1
- Psalm 33:5
- Psalm 67:5-6
- Psalm 85:11-12
- Psalm 104:24
- Deuteronomy 32:13
- Genesis 14:19
- Haggai 2:8
- Exodus 19:5
- Psalm 115:16

12. Hidden Treasures of Darkness
- Isaiah 45:3

13. Provision by Individuals
- Men—Luke 6:38; Psalms 68:29, 72:10, 112:5; Matthew 7:12; 2 Samuel 23:14-17
- Kings—Proverbs 21:1; Ezra 6:3-4, 7-8; 2 Chronicles 9:12; Esther 5:8
- Inheritance from relatives—Proverbs 19:14; 2 Corinthians 12:14

14. God Uses Us
- The power to get wealth—Deuteronomy 8:18; Proverbs 16:22; Genesis 24:35; Psalm 37:21-22
- Prayer of agreement—Matthew 18:18-20; 2 Kings 7:3, 5-6
- Thanksgiving—Philippians 4:6
- Work—Ephesians 4:28; 2 Thessalonians 3:10; Proverbs 6:6, 10:5, 12:11, 13:11, 14:23, 20:13; Romans 12:11
- Hand of the diligent makes rich—Proverbs 10:4, 12:24
- Thoughts of the diligent—Proverbs 21:5
- Being faithful—Luke 16:10-12, 19:17
- Being generous—1 Timothy 6:17-19
- Developing an established heart—Psalm 112:5-8
- Fasting—Matthew 6:17-18; Isaiah 58:6-8
- Confession—Proverbs 10:20, 12:18, 15:4, 18:21

15. Witty Inventions
- Proverbs 8:12

16. Simply the World's System
- The wicked and the sinner—Proverbs 13:22; Ecclesiastes 2:26; James 5:1-3
- Stolen goods returned—Exodus 22:1; Psalm 79:12; Proverbs 6:30-31, 22:22-23
- Steal it back from the enemy—Exodus 3:21-22, 12:36; 2 Chronicles 20:25; 2 Kings 7:8; Joshua 12:1, 13:1; Isaiah 53:12; 1 Samuel 30:19
- Other nations—Isaiah 61:5, 60:5

17. Angels
- Psalm 103:20-21
- 2 Kings 6:17
- Hebrews 1:14

18. Wildlife
A man shared several years ago of how he spoke to the birds to bring him money. Based upon 1 Kings 17, he said he started finding money outside around the house after he went out and hollered at the birds. They gathered around and listened to him. "People lose money every day. Go get it!"

A 15-year-old was so impressed with this story, he decided to try it. He asked the Lord for $10 for missions and God provided seed to the sower.

He went out and spoke to the birds, commanding them to put it in a tree in the backyard:

    Day 1 $1.65
    Day 2 $2.35
    Day 3 $7
    Day 4 $10

Over the next two months, he found $440 in the tree.

- 1 Kings 17:4-6
- Matthew 17:27
- Genesis 22:13-14
- Psalm 50:10

19. Because the Lord Needs It
- Mark 14:13-16
- Mark 11:2-3

20. Our Covenant Inheritance
- The Blessing of Abraham—Galatians 3:13-14
- The righteous will never beg for bread—Psalm 37:25
- Through faith and patience—Hebrews 6:12; James 1:3-5
- Our prosperous lineage—Genesis 17:1-2
- Inheritance through being a joint heir with Jesus—Galatians 3:29; Ephesians 1:10-11; Romans 8:16-17; Psalm 37:18

21. The Favor of God
- Exodus 11:3
- Deuteronomy 33:23
- Joshua 11:20
- 1 Samuel 16:22
- Esther 2:17
- Esther 5:8
- Esther 8:5

GLORIA COPELAND & PASTOR GEORGE PEARSONS

Our Supernatural Provider

DAY #2

A. **Philippians 4:19—Our Source of Our Supply**

   1. AMP/GK: "My God will liberally supply, fill to the full, cram, furnish, satisfy, finish and complete all of your needs, employment, requirements, lack and business according to His riches, His wealth, His money and His possessions in Glory by Christ Jesus."

      a. "Heaven always has a good economy. That's where we receive from. It doesn't matter what's happening in the earth—we're not receiving from the earth. We're receiving from heaven. It's like we're already there because heaven is our home. We live in a heaven reality. We are in the flesh on the earth, but we live by the spirit." —Gloria Copeland

      b. Psalm 23:5: "...my cup runneth over."

   2. Settle this today: God is my Supernatural Source!

   3. *Source*—the point of origin, the beginning place

   4. 1 Corinthians 8:6 (AMP): "Yet for us there is [only] one God, the Father, Who is the Source of all things and for Whom we [have life], and one Lord, Jesus Christ, through and by Whom are all things and through and by Whom we [ourselves exist]."

   5. "Don't look to the government for your supply. Don't look to other people for your supply. No, no. Pastors, don't look to your congregation for your supply. Jesus is our Source. The Blessing of Abraham is our supply. The Word is our supply."
   —Word from the Lord through Brother Copeland, Nov. 11, 2010

      a. "We found out it belongs to us, and we took what belongs to us."
      —Gloria Copeland

B. **Genesis 22:1-14—Jehovah Jireh—Our Supernatural Provider**
   1. Verses 7-8: "But where is the lamb for a burnt offering? And Abraham said, My son, God will provide himself a lamb for a burnt offering."
   2. Verse 13: "Abraham lifted up his eyes and looked, and behold behind him was a ram caught in a thicket by his horns: and Abraham went and took the ram, and offered him up for a burnt offering in the stead of his son."
      a. Lifting up our eyes is symbolic of our faith—looking to our Provider in faith, to God, to heaven, to the Word, to the supernatural, from the impossible into all things of the spirit.
   3. Verse 14: "And Abraham called the name of that place Jehovahjireh: as it is said to this day, In the mountain of the Lord, it shall be seen."
   4. CEV: "Abraham named that place, 'The Lord Will Provide.' And even now people say, 'On the mountain of the Lord it will be provided.'"
   5. MSG: "Abraham named that place God-Yireh (GOD-Sees-to-It). That's where we get the saying, 'On the mountain of God—he sees to it.'"

C. **The Lord God—My Supernatural Provider**
   1. One of the Names of God is "Provider."
      a. Everywhere you see His Name, add "my supernatural Provider" after it.
      b. This will renew your mind to God's supernatural provision.
   2. Deuteronomy 28:8,11-12 (AMP)—The Blessing of Abraham
      a. Verse 8: The Lord [my supernatural Provider] shall command The Blessing upon me in my storehouse and in all that I undertake. And He [my supernatural Provider] will bless me in the land which the Lord my God [my supernatural Provider] gives me.
      b. Verse 11: And the Lord [my supernatural Provider] shall make me have a surplus of prosperity, through the fruit of my body, of my livestock, and of my ground, in the land which the Lord [my supernatural Provider] swore to my fathers to give me.
      c. Verse 12: The Lord [my supernatural Provider] shall open to me His good treasury, the heavens, to give the rain of my land in its season and to bless all the work of my hands; and I shall lend to many nations, but I shall not borrow.
   3. Psalm 68:19: Blessed be the Lord [my supernatural Provider] who daily loads me with benefits, even the God [my supernatural Provider] of my salvation.
   4. 2 Corinthians 9:8 (AMP): And God [my supernatural Provider] is able to make all grace (every favor and earthly blessing) come to me in abundance, so that I may always and under all circumstances and whatever the need be self-sufficient [possessing enough to require no aid or support and furnished in abundance for every good work and charitable donation].
   5. Our supernatural Provider has unusual ways and unlimited avenues of providing that supersede all natural limitations.

God's Great Storehouse
WORD FROM THE LORD THROUGH KENNETH COPELAND, NOV. 10, 2011

"I have a great storehouse. Much more has been stored up in the storehouse of riches beyond your wildest dream that I laid up for you before the foundation of the world. Much more is stored up there than what the Church has ever called for. I never have held back on the Church," saith The LORD and the God of plenty. "I've made it available to you. I put it in My WORD. I gave you promise and stood behind it with the blood—the precious blood of your Savior.

"But there has been a backwardness in My people about laying hold of the things that I have provided for you.

"But I will say this: There is a people in the land. There is a people around the world. There is a people strong and mighty growing much stronger and much mightier and more bold to lay hold and put their claim of faith on the things that I have laid up for them and it thrills Me," saith The LORD, "because it's been theirs all the time."

NOTES

GLORIA COPELAND & PASTOR GEORGE PEARSONS

The Circle of Supernatural Provision

DAY #3

A. **Galatians 6:7-8—The Supernatural Act of Giving**

1. AMP: "For whatever a man sows, that and that only will he reap. For he who sows to his own flesh (lower nature, sensuality) will from the flesh reap decay and ruin and destruction, but he who sows to the Spirit will from the Spirit reap eternal life."

2. Tithing and sowing are supernatural acts.
    a. They are not natural.
    b. They are ordained by God.

3. The supernatural act of tithing and sowing will result in a supernatural harvest of supernatural provision in spite of economic conditions.
    a. "If you aren't tithing and sowing, you're not living in the supernatural. That circle is broken when you quit tithing and sowing." —Gloria Copeland

4. The harvest is always much greater when dealing with the supernatural realm.
    a. Tithing results in the open windows of heaven.
    b. Sowing results in the hundredfold return.

5. "Financial inversion shall increase in these days. For you see, it is My desire to move in the realm of your financial prosperity. But release Me," saith the Lord, "release Me that I may come in your behalf and move in your behalf. As men walk in My Word, so shall they walk in the ways of The Lord. Oh yes, there will be some who say, 'Yes, but God's ways are higher, surely higher than our ways, and we can't walk in those ways.' It's true that the ways of God are higher. They are higher than your ways as the heavens are above the earth, but I'll teach you to walk in My ways. I never did say you couldn't walk in My ways. Now learn to walk in it. Learn to give.

So shall the inversion of the financial system revert and so shall it be that the gospel of the kingdom shall be preached to all the world, and there shall be no lack in the kingdom. Those who give shall walk in the ways of the supernatural!"
—Word from the Lord through Charles Capps, Feb. 1, 1978.

B. Malachi 3:10-13—Tithing Is a Supernatural Act

1. Malachi 3:10-12 (AMP): "Bring all the tithes (the whole tenth of your income) into the storehouse, that there may be food in My house, and prove Me now by it, says the Lord of hosts, if I will not open the windows of heaven for you and pour you out a blessing, that there shall not be room enough to receive it. And I will rebuke the devourer [insects and plagues] for your sakes and he shall not destroy the fruits of your ground, neither shall your vine drop its fruit before the time in the field, says the Lord of hosts. And all nations shall call you happy and blessed, for you shall be a land of delight, says the Lord of hosts."

2. Genesis 14:20, 15:1 (AMP): After he tithed, "the word of the Lord came to Abram in a vision, saying, Fear not, Abram, I am your Shield, your abundant compensation, and your reward shall be exceedingly great."

3. Example: KCM was experiencing a $1 million deficit. In January of 1984, Brother Copeland went to their prayer cabin in Arkansas to seek The Lord. The answer came: "Tithe KCM's income—10 percent off the top." It was not the answer he was expecting, but he willingly obeyed and the financial situation turned around. This supernatural act of tithing produced supernatural provision for Kenneth Copeland Ministries.

C. 2 Corinthians 9:6-8 (AMP)—Sowing Is a Supernatural Act

1. Verse 6: "[Remember] this: he who sows sparingly and grudgingly will also reap sparingly and grudgingly, and he who sows generously [that blessings may come to someone] will also reap generously and with blessings."

2. Verse 7: "Let each one [give] as he has made up his own mind and purposed in his heart, not reluctantly or sorrowfully or under compulsion, for God loves (He takes pleasure in, prizes above other things, and is unwilling to abandon or to do without) a cheerful (joyous, "prompt to do it") giver [whose heart is in his giving]."

3. Verse 8: "And God is able to make all grace (every favor and earthly blessing) come to you in abundance, so that you may always and under all circumstances and whatever the need be self-sufficient [possessing enough to require no aid or support and furnished in abundance for every good work and charitable donation]."

4. Genesis 26:12-13 (NIV): "Isaac planted crops in that land and the same year reaped a hundredfold, because the Lord blessed him. The man became rich, and his wealth continued to grow until he became very wealthy."

5. Sowing is a supernatural act that produces supernatural provision.

NOTES

NOTES

GLORIA COPELAND & PASTOR GEORGE PEARSONS

Supernatural Provision in the Old Testament—Part 1

DAY #4

A. **Genesis 26:12-14—Supernatural Return (Isaac Reaped in Famine)**
   1. Psalm 37:18-19 (NLT): "Day by day the Lord takes care of the innocent, and they will receive an inheritance that lasts forever. They will not be disgraced in hard times; even in famine they will have more than enough."
      a. "The hundredfold return is never affected by the government or the times we live in." —Gloria Copeland
   2. This was a supernatural yield; even in the most fertile regions of Israel, the harvest was no greater than twenty-five to fiftyfold.
   3. Genesis 26:13 (NLT): "He became a very rich man, and his wealth continued to grow."
   4. Genesis 26:28-29: The men saw that THE BLESSING was on Isaac—they had to admit it!
   5. "If you're doing it right, THE BLESSING can be seen." —Gloria Copeland

B. **Exodus 16:11-15—Supernatural Supply (Wilderness Provisions)**
   1. Psalm 78:23-29 (NLT): "But he commanded the skies to open; he opened the doors of heaven. He rained down manna for them to eat; he gave them bread from heaven. They ate the food of angels! God gave them all they could hold. He released the east wind in the heavens and guided the south wind by his mighty power. He rained down meat as thick as dust—birds as plentiful as the sand on the seashore! He caused the birds to fall within their camp and all around their tents. The people ate their fill. He gave them what they craved."
   2. Deuteronomy 29:5 (AMP): "I have led you forty years in the wilderness; your clothes have not worn out upon you, and your sandals have not worn off your feet."
      a. Proverbs 8:17-21—Durable riches (verse 18)
   3. Deuteronomy 2:7 (NLT): "For the Lord your God has blessed you in everything you have done. He has watched your every step through this great wilderness. During these forty years, the Lord your God has been with you, and you have lacked nothing."

C. Leviticus 26:4-5, 9-10—Supernatural Harvest

1. Verse 9 (AMP): "For I will be leaning toward you with favor and regard for you, rendering you fruitful, multiplying you, and establishing and ratifying My covenant with you."

2. Verse 10 (MSG): "You'll still be eating from last year's harvest when you have to clean out the barns to make room for the new crops."
    a. NLT-96: "You will have such a surplus of crops that you will need to get rid of the leftovers from the previous year to make room for each new harvest."

3. Amos 9:13 (NLT): "'The time will come,' says the Lord, 'when the grain and grapes will grow faster than they can be harvested. Then the terraced vineyards on the hills of Israel will drip with sweet wine!'"
    a. MSG: "'Yes indeed, it won't be long now.' God's Decree. 'Things are going to happen so fast your head will swim, one thing fast on the heels of the other. You won't be able to keep up. Everything will be happening at once—and everywhere you look, blessings! Blessings like wine pouring off the mountains and hills.'"

D. 1 Kings 17:1-6—Supernatural Meals (Elijah Fed by Ravens)

1. Verse 4 (NKJV): "I have commanded the ravens to feed you."
    a. Matthew 10:29: "Are not two sparrows sold for a farthing? and one of them shall not fall on the ground without your Father?"

    b. *Fall* (GK) = shall not land without your Father's permission

2. "These provisions were ready prepared, the bread made and baked, and the flesh boiled, broiled, or roasted." (From *John Gill's Exposition of the Old Testament, Volume 2*)

3. A minister was sharing how he spoke to the birds to bring him money based upon 1 Kings 17. He began finding money around the house after he went outside and hollered at the birds. A 15-year-old was so impressed with this story that he decided to try it. He wanted $10.00 for missions. He went outside, spoke to the birds and commanded them to put the money in the backyard tree. Over the next two months, he collected $440.00 in the tree.

E. 1 Kings 17:8-16—Supernatural Provision (Continual Supply of Flour and Oil)

1. Verse 13: "Make me a cake first and bring it to me."
    a. Elijah activated her faith.

    b. He had her bring the tithe so he could bless it.

2. Verse 15: "She, and he, and her house, did eat *a full year*" (KJV cross-reference, *Kenneth Copeland Reference Edition Bible*).

3. Verse 16 (NLT-96): No matter how much they used, there was always enough left in the containers, just as the Lord had promised through Elijah.
    a. NIV: "For the jar of flour was not used up and the jug of oil did not run dry, in keeping with the word of the Lord spoken by Elijah."

NOTES

NOTES

GLORIA COPELAND & PASTOR GEORGE PEARSONS

Supernatural Provision in the Old Testament—Part 2

DAY #5

A. 1 Kings 19:4-8—Supernatural Sustenance (Food Sustained Elijah for 40 Days)

1. "The natural is limited to natural ways, but the supernatural is unlimited in supernatural ways." —Gloria Copeland

2. This kind of provision is available to all believers—especially when the situation, job market, paycheck, economy and others are saying, "There's no way to meet this need. It is humanly impossible."

3. "The stones hereabout might be heated by a supernatural power and the cake baked on them by an angel." —*John Gill's Exposition of the Old Testament, Volume 2*

4. Verse 8: "And he arose, and did eat and drink, and went in the strength of that meat forty days and forty nights unto Horeb the mount of God."

5. "All this while he had no other sustenance than what he had taken under the juniper tree, from whence he set out, which must be supernatural; for it is said a man cannot live without food beyond seven days, for food either staying in his stomach all this while, or however the nutritive virtue of it, by which he was supported and held out till he came to Horeb." —*John Gill's Exposition of the Old Testament, Volume 2*

B. 2 Kings 4:1-7—Supernatural Debt Cancellation (Widow Avoids Bankruptcy)

1. Verse 2: Elisha asked, "What do you have? Give me a seed to work with."

2. Verses 3-6: "Borrow as many pots as you can, pour into them until they are full and then pour into the next one." The oil stopped pouring when they ran out of pots.

3. Verse 7: She made enough money selling the oil that she paid the creditor, saved her children and lived the rest of her life off the remaining oil sale.

C. 2 Kings 4:42-44—Supernatural Multiplication (Food Multiplied to Feed 100)

1. Verse 42: He brought his tithe to the man of God to bless.

2. Verse 43 (NLT): "'What?' his servant exclaimed. 'Feed a hundred people with only this?' But Elisha repeated, 'Give it to the people so they can eat, for this is what the Lord says: Everyone will eat, and there will even be some left over!'"

3. Verse 44 (NLT): "And when they gave it to the people, there was plenty for all and some left over, just as the Lord had promised."

D. 2 Kings 7:1-2—Supernatural Acceleration (Tomorrow at This Time)

1. Verse 1: "To morrow about this time"—24 hours from now.

2. Verse 2 (NLT): "The officer assisting the king said to the man of God, 'That couldn't happen even if the Lord opened the windows of heaven!' But Elisha replied, 'You will see it happen with your own eyes, but you won't be able to eat any of it!'"
    a. What keeps us from the supernatural?
        i. Time—don't put what God has done off into the future.
        ii. Unbelief—the supernatural only operates by faith.

3. Verse 18—The famine was over 24 hours later.
    a. There was plenty for all.
    b. It was cheap.

E. Job 42:12-17—Supernatural Restoration (Job's Life Turned Around)

1. MSG: "God blessed Job's later life even more than his earlier life. He ended up with fourteen thousand sheep, six thousand camels, one thousand teams of oxen, and one thousand donkeys."

2. MSG: "He also had seven sons and three daughters. He named the first daughter Dove, the second, Cinnamon, and the third, Darkeyes. There was not a woman in that country as beautiful as Job's daughters. Their father treated them as equals with their brothers, providing the same inheritance."

3. MSG: "Job lived on another 140 years, living to see his children and grandchildren—four generations of them!"

NOTES

NOTES

LIVING IN THE REALM OF GOD'S SUPERABUNDANCE

GLORIA COPELAND & PASTOR GEORGE PEARSONS

Supernatural Provision in the New Testament

DAY #6

A. **Matthew 17:24-27—Supernatural Payment (Tax Relief)**

  1. Genesis 1:28—Have dominion over the fish of the sea.

  2. Jesus was operating in the word of knowledge.

  3. Isaiah 45:3 (MSG): "I will lead you to buried treasures, secret caches of valuables—confirmations that it is, in fact, I, God, the God of Israel, who calls you by your name."
     a. *Cache*—a collection of items stored in a hidden or inaccessible place

     b. Stockpile, supply, reserve, arsenal

B. **Mark 11, 14—Supernatural Transportation and Housing**

  1. Mark 11:1-6: "The Lord has need of this donkey."

  2. Mark 14:13-16—A furnished upper room

  3. Isaiah 55:1: "Ho, every one that thirsteth, come ye to the waters, and he that hath no money; come ye, buy, and eat; yea, come, buy wine and milk without money and without price."

C. **Luke 5:1-11—Supernatural Harvest (Great Catch of Fish)**

  1. This was the harvest from Jesus' use of Peter's boat.

  2. Peter didn't plan for the supernatural.
     a. He let down only one broken net.

     b. Faith plans for more than enough.

     c. If we are expecting the supernatural, we will get it.

3. Jesus stimulated the Galilee fishing industry.
    a. It was in a slump.
    b. That day, the fish market exploded!
    c. Peter's business was on the verge of bankruptcy.
    d. Jesus saw to it that the family business would thrive in Peter's absence as a disciple.

D. **John 2:1-11—Supernatural Replenishment (Water Into Wine)**
    1. Jesus supernaturally turned 180 gallons of water into wine.
    2. He supernaturally jumped the natural steps and dominated the time constraints of producing wine.
        a. Plant seed.
        b. Wait nine months for the vine to grow.
        c. Harvest the grapes.
        d. Mash the grapes.
        e. Let the wine ferment (the longer the time, the better the wine).
    3. Verse 10 (MSG): "You've saved the best till now!"
        a. A $320,000 bottle has been fermenting for 200 years!
        b. Jesus produced the best.
        c. The guests couldn't possibly drink it all.
        d. It was a wedding gift from Jesus.
        e. They would sell it and not have to work their first year.
    4. Genesis 1:28: Replenish the earth—if it runs out, fill it back up.
    5. John 2:11: This was the beginning of miracles—a supernatural intervention in the ordinary course of events.

E. **John 6:5-14—Supernatural Distribution (Five Thousand Fed)**
    1. Verse 5 (NLT): "Where can we buy bread to feed all these people?"
        a. Philip was limited in his believing.
        b. Verse 7 (NLT): "Even if we worked for months, we wouldn't have enough money to feed them."
        c. Jesus was teaching His disciples how to use their faith for supernatural provision.

2. Verse 11: Jesus distributed the loaves and fishes to the disciples, and the disciples distributed the loaves and fishes to the people.
    a. They were doing the same supernatural work as Jesus.
    b. They had the same faith Jesus had—to feed 20,000 people!
    c. Note the connection between thanksgiving and the supernatural.
3. "You are going to be the ones that God uses to supernaturally feed the lost when disasters come. Only, it is not going to be like it was in the past. In many cases, you are not even going to need the trucks and airplanes. In a lot of cases, you are just going to take one little meal and divide it and divide it and divide it." —Word from the Lord through Kenneth Copeland, Nov. 19, 2005.

NOTES

NOTES

SUPERNATURAL PROVISION
LIVING IN THE REALM OF GOD'S SUPERABUNDANCE

GLORIA COPELAND & PASTOR GEORGE PEARSONS

Supernatural Wealth Transfer

DAY #7

> "We are not natural people. We're **supernatural people.** We're born of God!"
> —Gloria Copeland

A. Proverbs 13:22—The Wealth of the Sinner Is Laid Up for the Just

"Financial Inversion Shall Increase in These Days" —Word from the Lord through Charles Capps, Feb. 1, 1978

1. "Financial inversion shall increase in these days. For you see, it is My desire to move in the realm of your financial prosperity. But release Me, saith the Lord, release Me that I may come in your behalf and move on your behalf.

2. "For yes, there shall be in this hour financial distress here and there. The economy shall go up and it will go down; but those who learn to walk in the Word, they shall see the prosperity of the Word come forth in this hour in a way that has not been seen by men in days past.

3. "Yes, there's coming a financial inversion in the world's system. It's been held in reservoirs of wicked men for days on end. But the end is nigh.

4. "Those reservoirs shall be tapped and shall be drained into the gospel of Jesus Christ.

5. "It shall be done in the time allotted and so shall it be that the Word of the Lord shall come to pass that the wealth of the sinner is laid up for the just."

B. Psalm 105:37: "He brought them forth also with silver and gold: and there was not one feeble person among their tribes."

"The Largest, Most Significant Wealth Transfer" —Word from the Lord through Kenneth Copeland, March 8, 2012

1. "The largest, most significant transfer of property, goods, wealth and people from the hands of the devil into the hands of God's people who are prepared to receive it.

2. "I am telling you, the biggest transfer of property in the history of mankind has just begun and it is swinging into….

3. "It has moved over into its final stage, saith The LORD.

4. "And those who will listen to Me and follow Me and trust Me—those who I have taught My WORD and have given the authority to walk in these things, it is the most outstanding thing that human eyes have ever seen.

5. "And the time is now. Your time has come. Your hour has come. So rise and do those things by faith that you know to do and all that belongs to heaven will come into your hands for your joy."

C. James 5:1-4—Last Days Wealth Transfer

Excerpts from "Supernatural Wealth Transfer" by Bill Winston

1. "[God is] restoring the earth back into the hands of its rightful owners, as well as restoring the power or Blessing to govern it. Because of Adam's sin, the earth was not in the hands of God's family. Now, God is working His redemptive plan to get it all back…what I refer to as a SUPERNATURAL transfer of wealth.

2. "As we get closer to our Lord's return, there is an invasion of the kingdom of heaven into this world—the imposing of God's will on the plans of the devil. Earthly systems, laws, rules, policies and values must now come in line with Heaven's order or Heaven's Government, the Government of the Kingdom of God. Psalm 103:19 (ESV)…. His kingdom rules over all.

3. "One of the major things coming in this hour is an EXPLOSION OF WEALTH in the Body of Christ. Through divine favor, witty inventions and the grace of giving, we are at the season of the greatest WEALTH TRANSFER in the history of this planet. There will be inventions that make the iPhone® seem like child's play.

4. "This is a prophetic time in history, the same as the 'set-time' that triggered the release of the children of Israel from Egyptian bondage. This is a season when, what happened then is happening now. It is a set-time or a season which is the consummation of something pledged or promised by God. The reservoirs of the wicked will now be drained, and as the Babylonian system of the world fails, the system of the Kingdom of God will prevail.

5. "We are even going to see money supernaturally transfer into the bank accounts of the people of God. Why the transfer of wealth? Mainly for the advancing of the kingdom and bringing in the end-time harvest of souls. God needs the wealth in our hands to fulfill the call that is on our lives for this generation—to reclaim what Jesus redeemed."

NOTES

NOTES

SUPERNATURAL PROVISION
LIVING IN THE REALM OF GOD'S SUPERABUNDANCE

GLORIA COPELAND & PASTOR GEORGE PEARSONS

Supernatural Debt Cancellation

DAY #8

A. **Luke 4:14-21—Three Ways God Supernaturally Removes Debt**
   1. He provides the finances.
   2. He removes the debt.
   3. He moves upon others.
      a. Faith never puts pressure on others.

B. **He Provides the Finances**
   1. 2 Kings 4:1-7 (NLT) "…sell the olive oil and pay your debts, and you and your sons can live on what is left over."
   2. Luke 5:1-11—Simon Peter's fishing business avoided bankruptcy after Jesus told him where to drop the nets.
   3. Matthew 17:24-27—Taxes were paid from money in a fish's mouth.

C. **He Removes the Debt**
   1. Nehemiah 5:1-13—Nehemiah canceled the debts of the poor Jews.
   2. Matthew 18:23-27—The king forgave his servant of the 10,000 talents.
   3. Matthew 6:12—Key point: Forgive us our debts as we forgive our debtors.
   4. Colossians 2:13-14 (AMP): Jesus "cancelled and blotted out and wiped away the handwriting of the note…with its legal decrees and demands. He set aside and cleared completely out of our way by nailing it to [His] cross."
   5. Luke 16:1-7—He reduces the debt.
      a. EMIC testimony—debt reduced 75 percent (from $6,500 down to $1,600)

D. He Moves Upon Others

1. Philemon 18-19 (AMP): "If he has done you any wrong in any way, or owes anything [to you], charge that to my account. I, Paul, write it with my own hand—I promise to pay it [in full]...."

2. Luke 10:30-37: The Samaritan took out two pence and gave them to the owner of the inn and said to him, "Take care of him. Whatever else you have to spend, I will pay it back in full when I return."

3. God is the One who moves upon a person—not you.
    a. Faith puts no pressure on others.
    b. Faith puts pressure on the Word of the covenant.
    c. Faith says, "God is my source."
    d. Luke 6:38—You give, and it will be given to you.

E. Word From the Lord Through Brother Copeland

July 9, 2007, Anaheim, Calif.

1. "The manifestation of THE BLESSING is at an all-time high. You are approaching a 'Blessing manifestation of glory' that is an explosion in ways and intensity that the human race has never seen before.

2. "THE BLESSING will surround you. THE BLESSING will encase you. You will learn to walk in the secret place of the Most High God, blessed in His Blessing, blessed in His glory, blessed in your comings, blessed in your goings and blessed in your pocketbook.

3. "All debt will have to get up and leave you the way leprosy left the lepers of old.

4. "Debt is financial sickness. It is financial leprosy. It is an attempt to do with the natural world's monies and abilities what I created THE BLESSING to do for you. Only, it is a burden and not a blessing. Debt is part of the curse.

5. "If you will begin to confess the Word, you will be shocked and thrilled at how quickly you will have the glory arise and drive the debt out of your life.

6. "If you will bring your tithe to Me and spend time with Me, tithing that tithe to Me, I will teach you and I will train you and I will show you how to be debt free. I will bless you beyond your means. I will bless you beyond your income. I will bless you beyond your salaries. I will bless you beyond anything you have ever known before. I will show you things that you have never heard of before.

7. "You will take advantage of those things and be financially blessed. I will bring such a financial blessing upon you that you won't have any idea where it came from. It has come to an explosive place.

8. "I am ready, saith the Lord, if you will begin to confess it, walk in it and make it a priority in your life. Then, the glory will manifest in the midst and you will give Me praise. I will come and visit you and together, we will have a grand time."

For further study, see *21 Days to Your Debt Freedom*, available at kcm.org.

"We're assuming that you're acting on the Word, believing the Word, saying the Word, acting on it. When we say 'you can live debt free,' you can't do it in your own strength. But if you **take the Word,** put it in your eyes and your ears, put it down **in your heart,** bring it out of your mouth, and have the patience to bring it forth, it'll come to pass. **It will come to pass!** But you can't just say, 'OK, I believe I'm going to be debt free' and it happen. It'll happen, but **you're going to have to use your faith.**"
—Gloria Copeland

NOTES

_____
_____
_____
_____
_____
_____
_____
_____
_____
_____
_____
_____
_____
_____
_____
_____

NOTES

SUPERNATURAL PROVISION
LIVING IN THE REALM OF GOD'S SUPERABUNDANCE

GLORIA COPELAND & PASTOR GEORGE PEARSONS

Receiving Your Supernatural House

DAY #9

*"A supernatural house is the best kind of house because it has **no debt.** Since it's supernatural, you might as well build what you want without sparing!"*

—Gloria Copeland

A. Ephesians 3:20—A Home Beyond Your Highest Dreams

1. AMP: "Now to Him Who, by (in consequence of) the [action of His] power that is at work within us, is able to [carry out His purpose and] do superabundantly, far over and above all that we [dare] ask or think [infinitely beyond our highest prayers, desires, thoughts, hopes, or dreams]."

2. A supernatural house is one that is, "superabundantly, far over and above all that you would dare ask or think—a home that is infinitely beyond your highest prayers, desires, thoughts, hopes or dreams."

3. Psalm 35:27 (AMP): "Let those who favor my righteous cause and have pleasure in my uprightness shout for joy and be glad and say continually, Let the Lord be magnified, Who takes pleasure in the prosperity of His servant."

4. The Lord cares about the kind of home you live in and takes great pleasure in your surroundings.
   a. Genesis 2:8 (AMP): "And the Lord God planted a garden toward the east, in Eden [delight]; and there He put the man whom He had formed (framed, constituted)."

   b. *Eden* (HEB)—the region of Adam's home; House of Pleasure, a place of luxury

5. The Garden of Eden was God's original intent for our earthly homes.
    a. Our homes should be a refuge.
    b. A supernatural place that ministers the life of God.

B. Isaiah 32:18—Your Supernatural House
1. NIV: "My people will live in peaceful dwelling places, in secure homes, in undisturbed places of rest."
    a. MSG: "My people will live in a peaceful neighborhood—in safe houses, in quiet gardens."
    b. NLT: "My people will live in safety, quietly at home. They will be at rest.
2. Psalm 107:7 (AMP): "He led them forth by the straight and right way, that they might go to a city where they could establish their homes."
    a. MSG: "He put your feet on a wonderful road that took you straight to a good place to live."
    b. There's an address looking for you!
3. 2 Samuel 7:27 (NIV): "Lord Almighty, God of Israel, you have revealed this to your servant, saying, 'I will build a house for you.'"
    a. "We began believing God for the perfect home when we lived in Tulsa, Okla., in 1968. At the same time, there was a lady in Fort Worth, Texas, who started building her home. It was several years before I saw that home, but the floor plan was exactly what we needed to meet our needs as a family. It was perfect for us. She began to build it at the very time we began to believe for it. God started to work immediately."
    b. After moving back to Fort Worth, Kenneth and Gloria looked at the house. The owners tried to sell it, even give it away—but it was given back.
    c. "They couldn't even give it away! That was our home!" —Excerpts from Gloria Copeland, *God's Will Is Prosperity*
    d. God begins to work on your behalf as soon as you release your faith. You release it when you pray.
4. 1 Chronicles 28:19 (MSG): "Here are the blueprints for the whole project as God gave me to understand it."
5. 2 Samuel 7:10 (NIV): "And I will provide a place for my people Israel and will plant them so that they can have a home of their own and no longer be disturbed. Wicked people will not oppress them anymore, as they did at the beginning."
    a. Psalm 18:19 (AMP): "He brought me forth also into a large place; He was delivering me because He was pleased with me and delighted in me."
    b. HEB—A roomy place with wide expanses
    c. NIV—A spacious place

C. **Psalm 112:1-3—Your Supernatural Furnishings**
   1. Kenneth Copeland, *From Faith to Faith—A Daily Guide to Victory*

      I'll never forget the time Gloria discovered that scripture. We didn't have any money at the time, and the walls in our house were as bare as they could be. But she was ready to decorate. So she took that promise, "Wealth and riches shall be in his house" and laid claim to it by faith.

      Suddenly, everywhere we went, somebody was giving us a painting or some other little treasure for our house.

      Unfortunately, most believers aren't as quick to believe God for that kind of thing as Gloria was. Some even claim God doesn't promise us New Testament believers physical prosperity, just spiritual. But the truth is, you can't separate the two. That's why Jesus says, "If you'll seek first the kingdom of God and His righteousness, then all these [material] things will be added to you." He knows the spiritual realm and the material realm are connected.

      The physical world cannot operate independently from the spiritual world. What happens in one is simply a reflection of what happens in the other.

      Obviously, your spiritual standing profoundly affects your financial standing. That's why, when you get hold of the gospel and begin to prosper spiritually, you can begin to prosper physically and materially as well.

      Don't let anyone talk you out of God's promises of prosperity. You don't have to choose between financial and spiritual prosperity. Both belong to you. Lay claim to them by faith. As a born-again child of God, dare to reach out and receive the riches that belong to you!

   2. Deuteronomy 6:10-11 (NIV): "When the Lord your God brings you into the land he swore to your fathers, to Abraham, Isaac and Jacob, to give you—a land with large, flourishing cities you did not build, houses filled with all kinds of good things you did not provide, wells you did not dig, and vineyards and olive groves you did not plant—then when you eat and are satisfied."
      a. Verse 11 (MSG): "Well-furnished houses you didn't buy."
      b. NLT: "The houses will be richly stocked with goods you did not produce."

   3. Proverbs 24:3-4 (NIV): "By wisdom a house is built, and through understanding it is established; through knowledge its rooms are filled with rare and beautiful treasures."
      a. Verse 4 (MSG): "It takes knowledge to furnish its rooms with fine furniture and beautiful drapes."
      b. NLT: "Through knowledge its rooms are filled with all sorts of precious riches and valuables."
      c. Proverbs 15:6 (AMP): "In the house of the [uncompromisingly] righteous is great [priceless] treasure."

NOTES

SUPERNATURAL PROVISION
LIVING IN THE REALM OF GOD'S SUPERABUNDANCE

GLORIA COPELAND & PASTOR GEORGE PEARSONS

Agents of Supernatural Provision

DAY #10

*You are going to be the ones God uses to **supernaturally feed the lost** when disasters come. Only, it is not going to be like it was in the past. In many cases, you are not even going to need the trucks and airplanes. In a lot of cases, you are just going to take one little meal and **divide it** and **divide it** and **divide it**.*

—Word from the Lord through Kenneth Copeland, Nov. 19, 2005

A. 2 Kings 4:42-44—The Man from Baal-Shalishah Became an Agent of Supernatural Provision

1. Verse 42 (NLT): "One day a man from Baal-shalishah brought the man of God a sack of fresh grain and twenty loaves of barley bread made from the first grain of his harvest. Elisha said, 'Give it to the people so they can eat.'"

2. Verse 43 (NLT): "'What?' his servant exclaimed. 'Feed a hundred people with only this?' But Elisha repeated, 'Give it to the people so they can eat, for this is what the Lord says: Everyone will eat, and there will even be some left over!'"
    a. "We have to get to the place where we can't even think lack." —Tommy Wilson

3. Verse 44 (NLT): "And when they gave it to the people, there was plenty for all and some left over, just as the Lord had promised."

4. Elisha used the man as an agent of supernatural provision.

5. Supernatural multiplication went through his hands for others.

B. John 6:5-11—The Disciples Became Agents of Supernatural Provision

1. NLT: "Then Jesus took the loaves, gave thanks to God, and distributed them to the people. Afterward he did the same with the fish. And they all ate as much as they wanted."

2. This translation (as well as others) is incorrect.

3. Jesus gave the fish and loaves to the disciples, and the disciples then distributed them to the people.

4. The disciples became part of the supernatural multiplication and distribution right along with Jesus.

5. The supernatural provision was going through their hands.

C. 2 Corinthians 9:8—We Are Agents of Supernatural Provision

1. There are two kinds of supernatural provision.
    a. Supernatural provision that is for us
    b. Supernatural provision that comes through us

2. Exodus 16—The children of Israel murmured and complained in the wilderness.
    a. They required manna and quail from heaven.
    b. They were relying on Moses' faith.

3. This is a time to develop our faith and grow up.
    a. We can't stay babies forever.
    b. We have to exercise our own faith.

4. There comes a time when we believe God to be "Agents of Supernatural Provision."
    a. We become distributors.
    b. Our motivation for accumulation is supernatural distribution.

5. 2 Corinthians 9:8 (AMP): "And God is able to make all grace (every favor and earthly blessing) come to you in abundance, so that you may always and under all circumstances and whatever the need be self-sufficient [possessing enough to require no aid or support and furnished in abundance for every good work and charitable donation]."
    a. We will supernaturally provide for others.
    b. We will supernaturally give a car to someone.
    c. We will supernaturally buy a home for someone.
    d. We will supernaturally pay off someone's debt.
    e. We will supernaturally multiply "fish and loaves" during times of crisis.

Supernatural Provision Confession
LIVING IN THE REALM OF GOD'S SUPERABUNDANCE

I am thriving—
not just surviving.

I am flourishing—
and not failing.

I believe I receive
supernatural provision,
an unlimited, overwhelming
supply that comes from above.

Provision is coming to me
from a higher place,
in a higher way,
from God's riches in glory.

I am not limited
to this natural world.

I expect God to provide.
I believe all things are possible.

My mind is being renewed
to His supernatural provision,
because He is
my supernatural Provider.

In Jesus' Name!

NOTES

THE SECRET TO SUPERNATURAL LIVING
BY KENNETH COPELAND

The LORD once said something to my good friend and preaching buddy Bill Winston that I'm convinced every one of us needs to hear. *Bill*, He said, *slow down…listen* for *Me and listen* to *Me*.

Those are simple but profound instructions we'd all do well to follow.

I've been reminded of that in recent months as I've been studying the words and life of Jesus. I've seen again and again that when He was on earth, hearing and obeying the Father was essential to His success.

This is the secret to supernatural living! Take the time to listen to the Father who is dwelling within you. Inquire of Him.

It's essential to ours, too. If we want to live the kind of supernatural life that Jesus lived, we must slow down enough to listen *for* and *to* our Father's voice.

"Oh, Brother Copeland!" you might say, "There's no way I can ever live like Jesus!"

Why not? You're His disciple, aren't you?

"Well, yes, but that doesn't mean I can actually be like Him."

According to Jesus it does. He said, "He that believeth on me, the works that I do shall he do also; and greater works than these shall he do; because I go unto my Father" (John 14:12). He also said, "If ye continue in my word, then are ye my disciples indeed; and ye shall know the truth, and the truth shall make you free" (John 8:31-32).

The very word *disciple* means, "to follow a teacher in order to become like him." I found that out firsthand when I started learning to fly airplanes. As an aspiring pilot, I became a "disciple" of my flight instructor. I didn't say, "I could never fly like he does." On the contrary, I fully expected to learn how to duplicate his expertise in the cockpit.

That was the whole idea! If I didn't duplicate him, I knew I'd wind up sticking the airplane in the ground like a dart. Since that's a good way to get killed, I made up my mind right away to follow my instructor's example.

He'd take the controls and say, "OK, I've got the airplane. Here's what we're going to do. You follow me through this." While he went through the maneuver, I'd rest my hands on the controls lightly, without putting any pressure on them, so I could sense what he was doing. When he finished, he'd say, "Now, it's your airplane. You take it." And I'd do my best to perform the maneuver exactly the same way.

Sure enough, I eventually learned to fly just like him.

We can apply the same principle to following Jesus. If we'll say what He said and do what He did, we'll get the same results He got.

I realize that idea upsets religious folks. They think it's blasphemous. "How dare you try to act like Jesus!" they say. "He's God!"

Certainly He is. But He didn't operate as God when He was on earth. As Philippians 2:7 says, He laid aside all the divine power that belonged to Him as a member of the Trinity and operated as a man. In other words, Jesus was as dependent on the power of His heavenly Father for His success in life and ministry as you and I are today. He said: "I do nothing of myself; but as my Father hath taught me, I speak.... And he that sent me is with me: the Father hath not left me alone; for I do always those things that please him. The words that I speak unto you I speak not of myself: but the Father that dwelleth in me, he doeth the works" (John 8:28-29, 14:10).

This is how Jesus lived: He said only what He heard His Father say. He did what His Father taught Him to do. Then, His Father supplied the power and did the miraculous works everyone marveled over.

That process brought Jesus 100-percent success all the time in every area of His life. If you'll duplicate it, it will do the same for you.

SUPERNATURALLY EMPOWERED IN EVERY AREA OF LIFE

"**B**ut I'm not really called to be a preacher," you might say. "So I don't need any miraculous power working in my life."

Yes, you do.

It's not just preachers who are supposed to have supernatural signs following them. Jesus didn't say that *preachers* would cast out demons, lay hands on the sick, do the works He did and even greater works. He said those things would be done by *those who believe*. (See Mark 16:17-18.)

If you're a believer, you are called to live a supernatural life—and not just when it comes to things like praying and sharing the gospel.

As your Lord and Savior, Jesus is committed to empowering you in every area—spirit, soul, body, finances, relationships and everything else that pertains to life and godliness. As your divine Source and Shepherd, He is responsible for your overall success just as His heavenly Father was responsible for His overall success when He was on earth.

How does Jesus carry out that responsibility?

By using the process I just outlined. He speaks the words of the Father to you through the written WORD and the Holy Spirit. He tells you what the Father has planned for you, what He has said about you, and what He has laid up for you. As you hear those words, speak them and obey them, the supernatural power of the Father goes to work in every area of your life.

"That's fine for people like you, Brother Copeland, and for Brother Winston, but the Holy Spirit doesn't ever say anything to me!"

I know you wouldn't purposely lie to me, but either you or Jesus—one or the other—isn't telling the truth, because Jesus said this to all of us who believe: "The Comforter, which is the Holy Ghost,  whom the Father will send in my name, he shall teach you all things, and bring all things to your remembrance, whatsoever I have said unto you. When he, the Spirit of truth, is come, he will guide you into all truth: for he shall not speak of himself; but whatsoever he shall hear, that shall he speak.... for he shall receive of mine, and shall show it unto you" (John 14:26, 16:13-14).

I've learned this from experience: When we, as believers, aren't hearing the Holy Spirit, it's not because He isn't speaking. It's because we need to clean out our spiritual ears. We've been so spiritually dense we haven't been hearing Him.

> Whether we're listening or not, **He's talking to us** in good times and bad times.

God is never an absentee Father. He is always there, speaking to us, teaching us and guiding us. Whether we're listening or not, He's talking to us in good times and bad times.

When the terrorists attacked on Sept. 11, 2001, for instance, He spoke to every human being in the Twin Towers and every person on those airplanes. Some heard what He said, acted on it and are still alive today as a result.

Gloria and I have friends who pastor a church on Wall Street. Most of their members work in or around those towers, but not a single one was hurt or killed in the attacks. One man was coming in the door of one of the towers just before the first plane crashed into it and he heard the Holy Ghost holler, *Run!* The man didn't stop to ask questions. (If he had, he would have been dead.) He just whirled around, ran down the street and into the subway tunnel to safety.

Another church member was already in the tower when the airplane hit. He followed the leading of the Holy Spirit and just walked out the front door calm as could be. Debris was falling all around him but he came out without any ashes on his clothes or even the smell of smoke.

That's the kind of thing that can happen when we're aware of what God's saying.

THE HAPPIEST MAN IN VIETNAM

Actually, no matter what God commands us to do—whether it's preaching in a church, teaching a kindergarten class, serving in the military, raising children at home or praying for a neighbor to be healed—He authorizes and empowers us to do it supernaturally.

One of my closest friends found that out in an amazing way years ago when he was flying an F-100 in Southeast Asia during the Vietnam War. Although he later went into the ministry, back then he didn't know much about faith or how to hear from God. He was a praying man, though, and he knew God had called him to do what he was doing at that particular time. So he continually trusted God to keep him safe.

One night he started having a recurring dream about a particularly dangerous mission. Night after night, it interrupted his sleep. He dreamed it over and over for months. "When the dream finally stopped coming, I was the happiest man in Vietnam," he told me. "I was thrilled to get some rest."

A few weeks later, his squadron was given a high-risk assignment. During the briefings, they were informed that the casualty potential was 50 percent. But when the mission commenced, my friend suddenly realized he already knew everything about it.

"I knew the location of the enemy troops," he said. "I knew where their gun emplacements were so I was able to warn my guys about them. A couple of our pilots went down but I knew exactly where they were and I was able to direct rescue and get them out. It didn't dawn on me until about halfway through the mission that I was flying that dream!"

In the end, his squadron not only completed their mission successfully, they did it without suffering any casualties.

That's how we, as believers, are meant to live! God won't necessarily speak to us through dreams. (He did that for my friend because he was a relatively young believer at that time.) He'll primarily speak to our hearts through the written WORD and the leading of the Holy Spirit. But to benefit from what He is saying to us, we have to slow down...listen *for* Him and listen *to* Him.

That kind of listening is another thing I learned about when I started flying airplanes. The first time I heard my flight instructor talking to ground control on the radio, I couldn't understand a thing the controller was saying. It sounded like gibberish to me. "What did he say?" I asked my instructor.

"He told us to taxi to runway 1-7," he answered.

A week or so later, after I began to learn a few things, I was preparing for takeoff in the little Cessna I flew back then and I had a different experience. I called ground control, identified myself to the controller, told him where I was and what I wanted. Because I'd begun to get acquainted with the process, I had some idea of what he was going to say back to me. As a result, I was able to hear and understand him.

If you're trying to hear from God and you don't know The WORD, you're going to feel like I did when I heard ground control for the first time. You're going to have a hard time understanding what God is saying to you because you aren't acquainted with how He talks. You don't know what to listen for.

Most likely, you'll be expecting Him to say something religious. But He doesn't talk religion! He speaks in line with His written WORD. He speaks faith, hope and love. He speaks THE BLESSING language. The more familiar you get with that language, the easier it will be for you to identify God's voice and discern what He's saying.

Even then, however, you'll have to train yourself to listen for Him.

In my early days as a pilot, one of the first things I learned to listen for was the tail number on my plane—55 X-ray—so I'd be sure to hear when the controller called it. That was important even back when I was flying in at 65 or 70 mph. These days it's even more vital. When I'm flying into places like New York City where planes are lined up, all of them flying 250 mph or more, I have to hear my number the moment it's called.

So what do I do? I listen for my instructions from the controller: I listen to them and I instantly obey.

That's what we all should be doing with the voice of The LORD!

As He told Brother Bill, we need to slow down and listen *for* Him and *to* Him. We need to take the time to do what He tells us to do in Psalm 46:10: "Be still, and know that I am God."

This is the secret to supernatural living! Take the time to listen to the Father who is dwelling within you. Inquire of Him. Ask Him to train your ear. He'll teach you His voice. He'll teach you how to follow Jesus and become His disciple.

Before long, you'll begin to realize He is leading you and placing you in the same position Jesus was in when He was on earth. You'll realize He is doing His works in your life. He's moving supernaturally for you in certain situations and places, manifesting Himself according to John 14:21.

Because God is absolutely righteous (which simply means He is absolute rightness) when He manifests Himself, things in your life start working right. Like an engine that's operating exactly like it's designed to operate, your life runs smoothly!

When people ask how you do it, you can answer like Jesus did. You can say, "I don't make it work, I just pray and obey. I just listen for and to the voice of my Shepherd, say what He says, and do what He tells me to do. Then the Father dwelling in me does the works."

That's what it means to be a disciple of Jesus. It means He commands, authorizes and empowers you. All you have to do is go!